Contents

Say the sounds

w x y qu ch sh th ng

Rings and things

I am Tim. This box is for my mum.

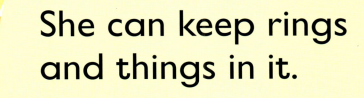

She can keep rings
and things in it.

3

Make the box

You can make a box too!

pens

card

egg box

foil

Get an egg box, pens, foil and card.

This box is quick to make.

Fix up the box

You can add all of this, too.

Fix the card to the top of the box.

Make the foil into tabs.

Fix the tabs onto the box.
Check that the box shuts.

Now get going with the pens.

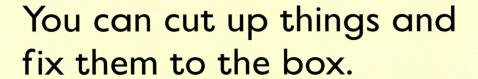

You can cut up things and fix them to the box.

11

You can fix pom-poms or buttons to the box.

pom-poms

buttons

I am fixing ribbons to my box.

Finish it off!

Now I will finish it off with shells.

A kiss, a box and a card for Mum!

The box looks good!

Glossary

 buttons

 card

 egg box

 foil

 pens

 pom-poms

 ribbons

 rings

 shells

 tabs